HOW TO USE THIS BOOK:

1. Take this Journal and a few pencils outside with you.
2. Look for something inspiring, interesting, or familiar to draw every day.
3. Some days you may want to write a poem or story about nature, animals, the weather, or your feelings.
4. You don't need to use the pages in order, use the page that you want to use each day.

THINGS TO THINK ABOUT WHEN YOU GO OUTSIDE:

1. Think about how each season brings change.
2. Think about how the sky and clouds look.
3. Think about how the weather feels.
4. Think about the sounds you hear in nature.
5. Think about the animals that live near you.
6. Think about the habitats of each living creature.
7. Think about the way nature looks at different times of day.
8. Think about the way your yard changes every month.
9. Think about how to draw every detail.
10. Think about how you can do your best to appreciate, protect, and respect the environment around you.

dyslexiefont.com

MY NAME:

Age: Date:

By: Sarah Janisse Brown

We use the Dyslexie Font by Christian Boer

With Drawings by Vanya Romanenko

Inspired by: Serena Marie Lapointe

The Thinking Tree Publishing Company, LLC

FUNSCHOOLINGBOOKS.COM

Copyright 2017 ~ Do Not Copy

Nature Hunt

Look at the pictures on the next page. When you go outside you can hunt for each item that you see on the page. When you find each item you may color it in.

Be patient. It may take a whole year to see everything!

MY BOOKS ABOUT ANIMALS & NATURE:

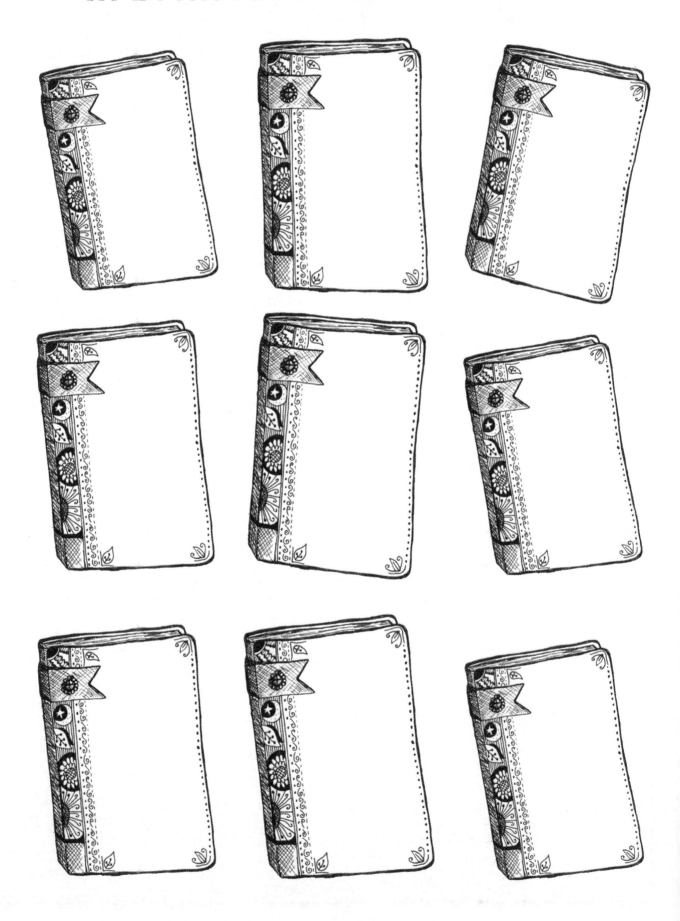

MY LEARNING LIST
Additional Books & Documentaries

TITLE: DATE:

BRING SOME NATURE INTO YOUR HOME

MAKE A NATURE STUDY BASKET

LIST THE ANIMALS THAT LIVE IN YOUR AREA:

_____
_____
_____
_____
_____
_____
_____
_____
_____
_____
_____
_____
_____
_____
_____

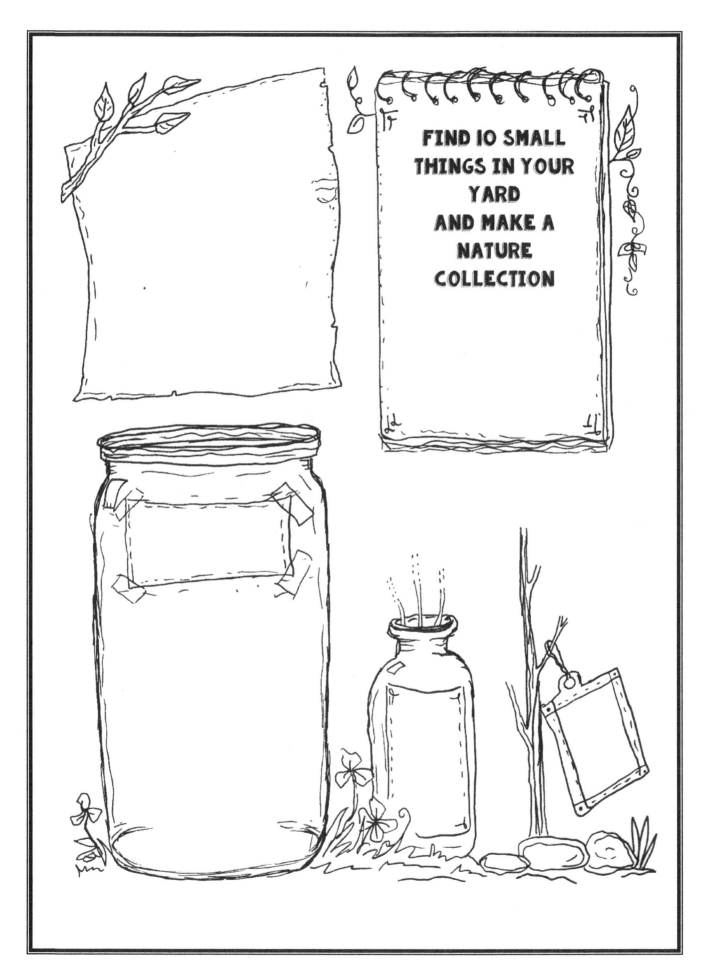

Today's Date:

COLOR ME
DRAW MY FOOD & HABITAT

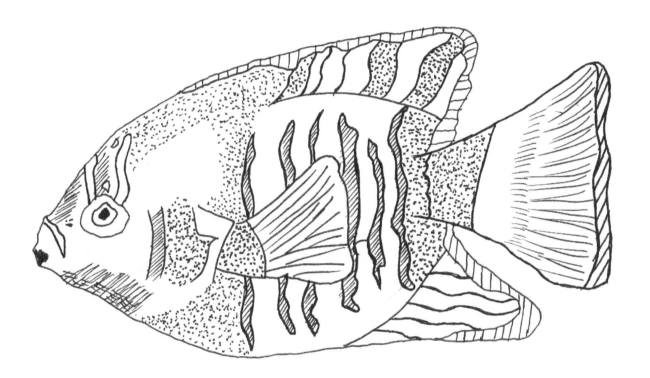

STUDY THE CLOUDS AND THE WEATHER

DRAW THE CLOUDS AND THE WEATHER

SPELLING TIME

Choose a Plant or Animal & Draw it Below

_____

Look in your nature books for 5 words that have some of the same letters as this plant or animal.

1. _____
2. _____
3. _____
4. _____
5. _____

CHANGING WITH THE SEASONS
DRAW A _____

Show how it changes with each season.

RESEARCH YOUR FAVORITE INSECT

NATURE NOTES, QUOTES AND POETRY

DRAW WHAT YOU SEE OUTSIDE TODAY

USE A CAMERA TO TAKE PICTURES OF NATURE

Print your photos and place them here:

COLLECT 10 SMALL THINGS FROM YOUR YARD AND MAKE A NATURE CRAFT.

DRAW A PICTURE TO ILLUSTRATE THIS POEM

August

No wind, no bird. The river flames like brass.
On either side, smitten as with a spell
Of silence, brood the fields. In the deep grass,
Edging the dusty roads, lie as they fell
Handfuls of shriveled leaves from tree and bush.
But 'long the orchard fence and at the gate,
Thrusting their saffron torches through the hush,
Wild lilies blaze, and bees hum soon and late.
Rust-colored the tall straggling briar, not one
Rose left. The spider sets its loom up there
Close to the roots, and spins out in the sun
A silken web from twig to twig. The air
Is full of hot rank scents. Upon the hill
Drifts the noon's single cloud, white, glaring, still.

Lizette Woodworth Reese

LEARN ABOUT NATURE, WEATHER OR ANIMALS ON A DIFFERENT CONTINENT

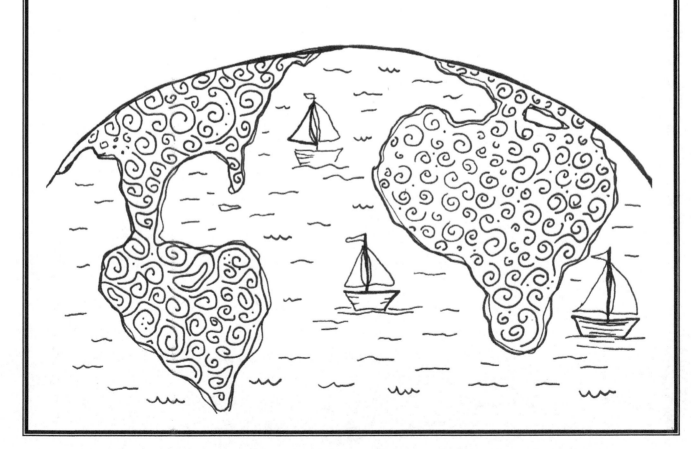

PLANTS OF THE WORLD

What plant are you learning about?

_____

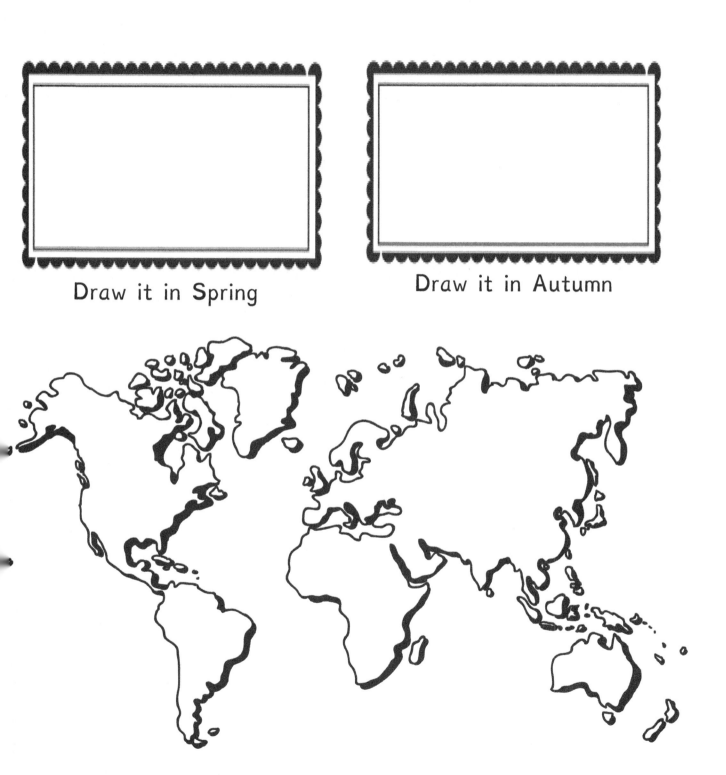

Draw it in Spring   Draw it in Autumn

Color the parts of the world where this plant lives.

Today's Date:
_____

READING TIME

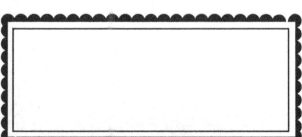

COLOR ME
DRAW MY FOOD & HABITAT

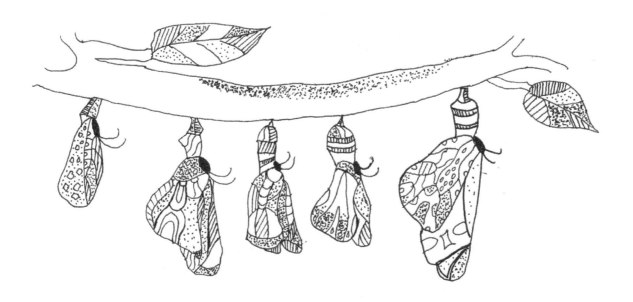

COLLECT 10 SMALL THINGS FROM NATURE AND MAKE A NATURE CRAFT.

DRAW SMALL THINGS YOU SEE OUTSIDE

SPELLING TIME

Choose a Plant or Animal & Draw it Below

_____

Look in your nature books for 5 words that have some of the same letters as this plant or animal.

1. _____
2. _____
3. _____
4. _____
5. _____

CHANGING WITH THE SEASONS
DRAW A _____
Show how it changes with each season.

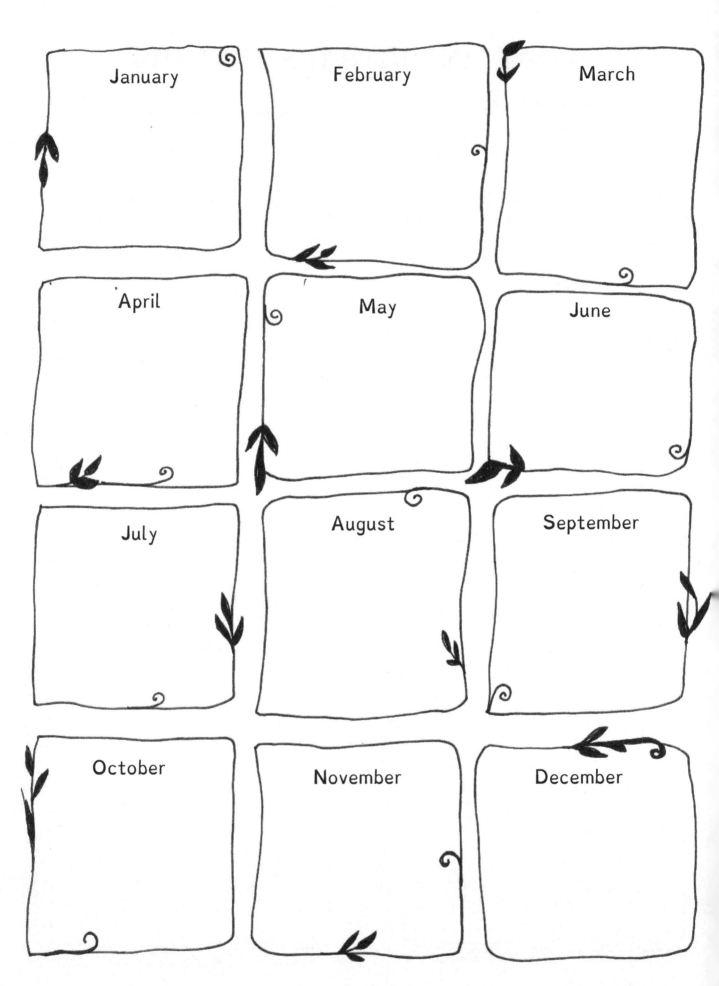

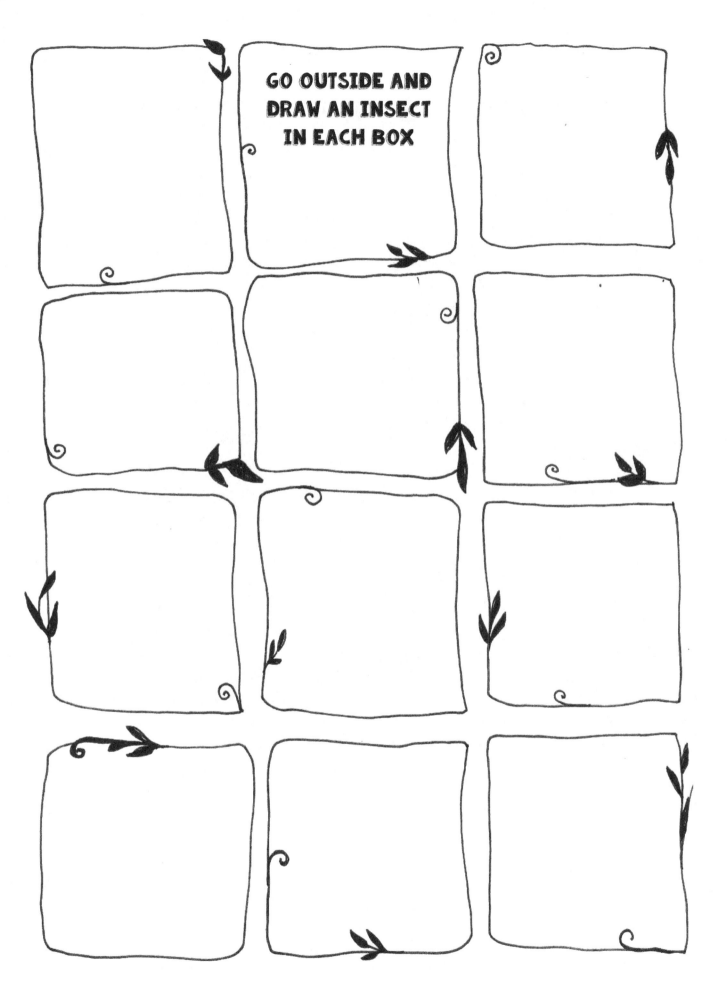

LEARN MORE ABOUT BUTTERFLIES

Five Facts About Butterflies:

1._____
2._____
3._____
4._____
5._____

READ A BOOK ABOUT THE ANIMALS THAT LIVE IN WATER.

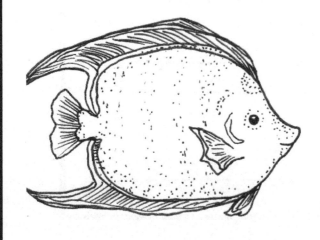

LEARN ABOUT NATURE, WEATHER OR ANIMALS ON A DIFFERENT CONTINENT

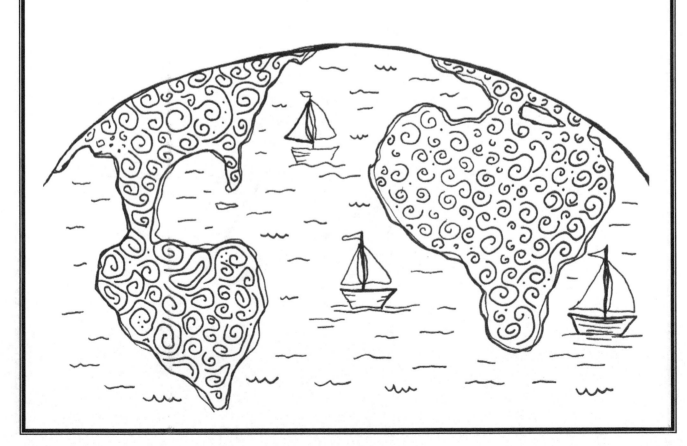

PLANTS OF THE WORLD

What plant are you learning about?

_____

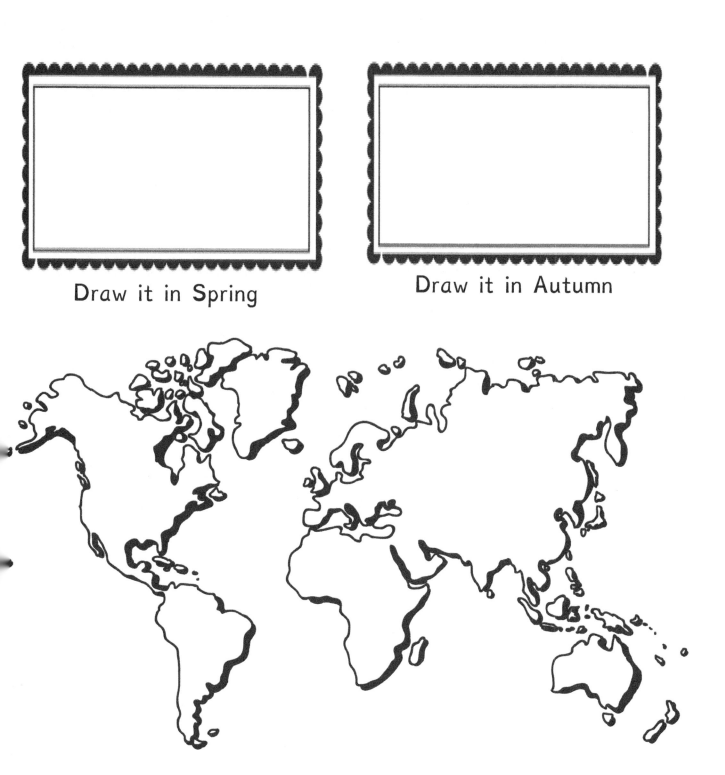

Draw it in Spring

Draw it in Autumn

Color the parts of the world where this plant lives.

COLLECT 10 SMALL THINGS FROM NATURE AND MAKE A NATURE CRAFT.

DRAW A PICTURE TO ILLUSTRATE THIS POEM

The Daffodils

I wandered lonely as a cloud
That floats on high o'er vales and hills,
When all at once I saw a crowd,
A host, of golden daffodils;
Beside the lake, beneath the trees,
Fluttering and dancing in the breeze.

William Wordsworth

MOVIE TIME

Watch a movie or documentary about nature.
TITLE:_____

VOCABULARY BUILDING

Look in your Nature & Animal Books for **FOUR** words with more than **TEN** letters. Write the words and their definitions below:

USE A CAMERA TO TAKE PICTURES OF NATURE

Print your photos and place them here:

Today's Date:
_____

READING TIME

COLOR ME
DRAW MY FOOD & HABITAT

COLLECT 10 SMALL THINGS FROM YOUR YARD AND MAKE A NATURE CRAFT.

DRAW SMALL THINGS YOU SEE OUTSIDE

DRAW A PICTURE TO ILLUSTRATE THIS POEM

I Meant to do My Work Today

I meant to do my work today—
But a brown bird sang in the apple tree,
And a butterfly flitted across the field,
And all the leaves were calling me.

And the wind went sighing over the land,
Tossing the grasses to and fro,
And a rainbow held out its shining hand—
So what could I do but laugh and go?

Richard Le Gallienne

RESEARCH YOUR FAVORITE FLOWER

ANIMAL TRACKS

CAT   JAGUAR   LION   TIGER

DOG   FOX   WOLF   BEAR

SHEEP   COW   HORSE   DEER

KANGAROO   LIZARD   HIPPOPOTAMUS   ELEPHANT

HOW MANY ANIMAL TRACKS CAN YOU DRAW?

LEARN MORE ABOUT TREES

Five Facts About Trees:

1._____
2._____
3._____
4._____
5._____

SPELLING TIME

Choose a Plant or Animal & Draw it Below

_____

Look in your nature books for 5 words that have some of the same letters as this plant or animal.

1. _____
2. _____
3. _____
4. _____
5. _____

CHANGING WITH THE SEASONS
DRAW A _____
Show how it changes with each season.

LEARN ABOUT NATURE, WEATHER OR ANIMALS ON A DIFFERENT CONTINENT

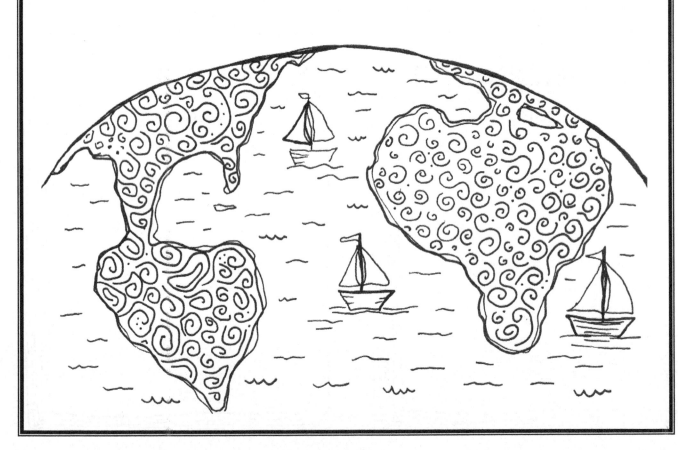

ANIMALS OF THE WORLD

What animal are you learning about?
_____

Draw a Male

Draw a Female

Color the parts of the world where this animal lives.

Today's Date:
_____
_____

READING TIME

COLOR ME
DRAW MY FOOD & HABITAT

USE A CAMERA TO TAKE PICTURES OF NATURE

Print your photos and place them here:

DRAW A PICTURE TO ILLUSTRATE THIS POEM

"Come, little leaves," said the wind one day,
"Come over the meadows with me, and play;
Put on your dresses of red and gold;
Summer is gone, and the days grow cold"
–from Songs of Autumn

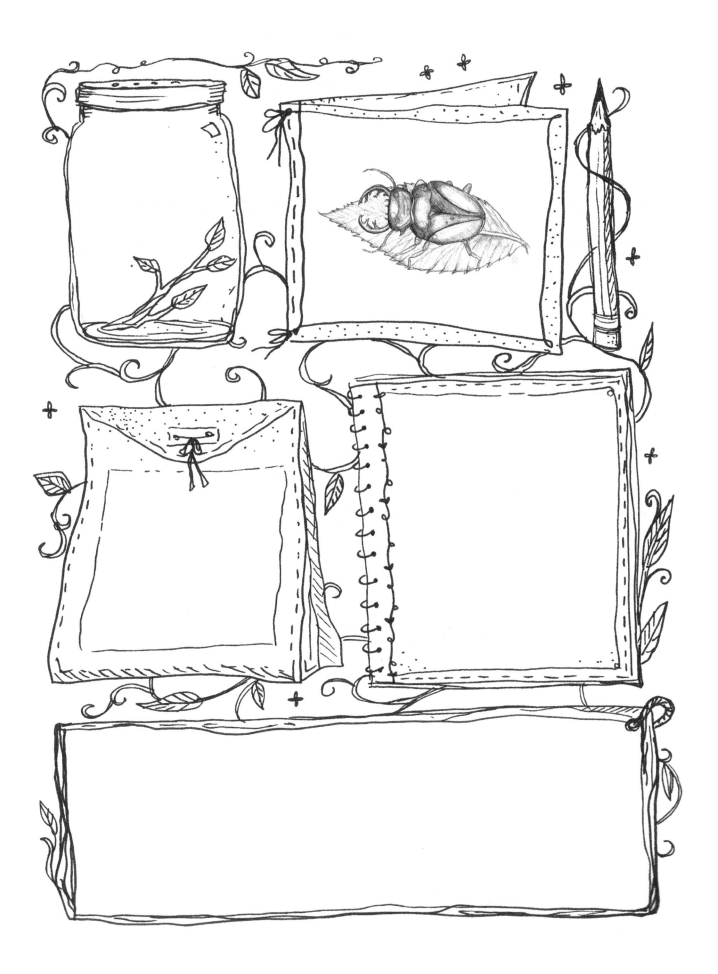

MOVIE TIME

Watch a movie or documentary about nature.
TITLE:_____

VOCABULARY BUILDING

Look in your Nature & Animal Books for **FOUR** words with more than **TEN** letters. Write the words and their definitions below:

COLLECT 10 SMALL THINGS FROM NATURE AND MAKE A NATURE CRAFT.

DRAW A PICTURE TO ILLUSTRATE THIS POEM

Sonnet 60

Like as the waves make towards the pebbled shore,
So do our minutes hasten to their end;
Each changing place with that which goes before,
In sequent toil all forwards do contend.

William Shakespeare

SPELLING TIME

Choose a Plant or Animal & Draw it Below

_____

Look in your nature books for 5 words that have some of the same letters as this plant or animal.

1. _____
2. _____
3. _____
4. _____
5. _____

CHANGING WITH THE SEASONS
DRAW A _____

Show how it changes with each season.

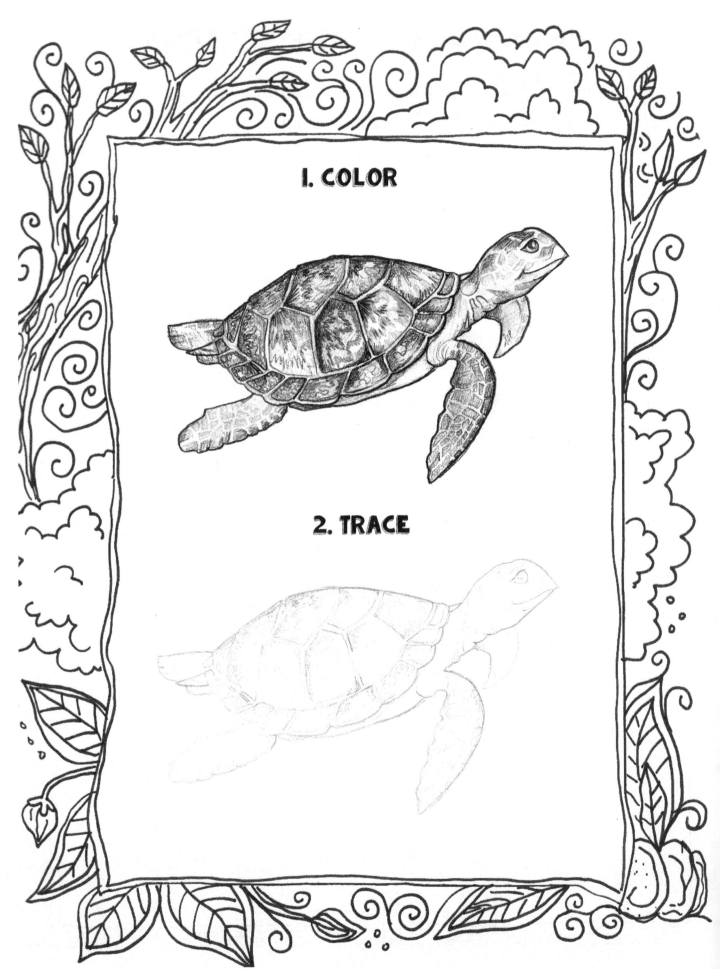

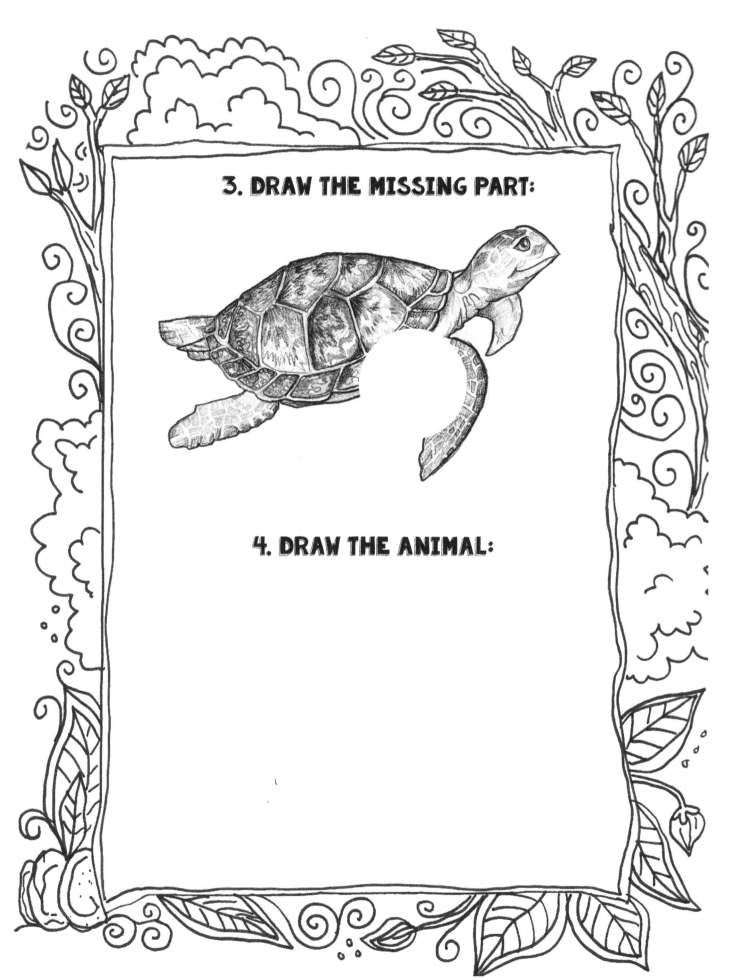

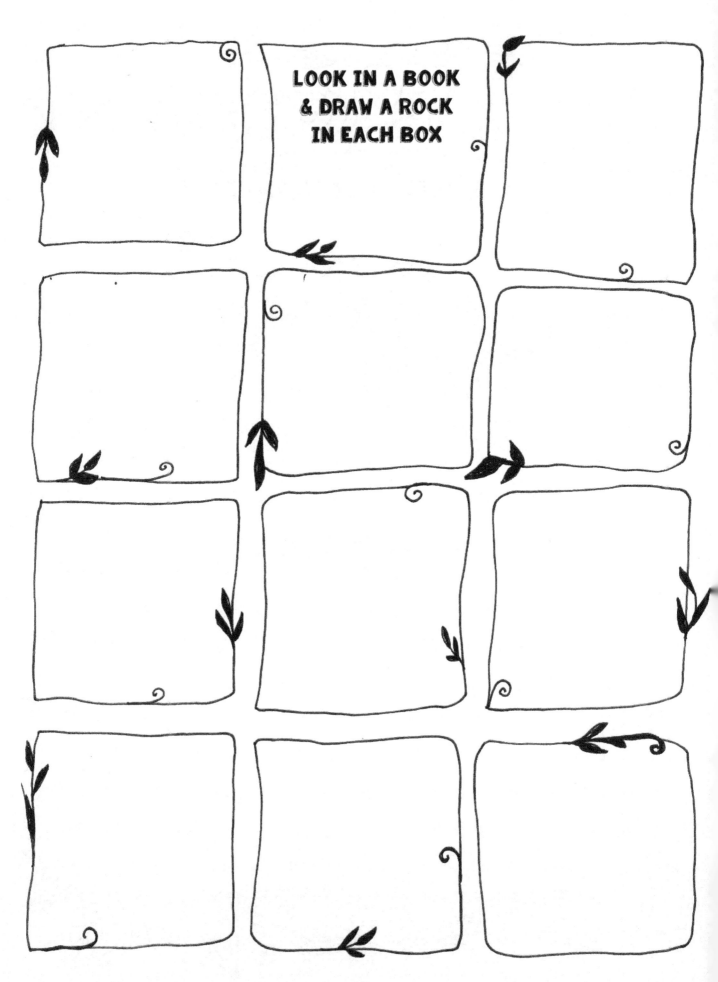

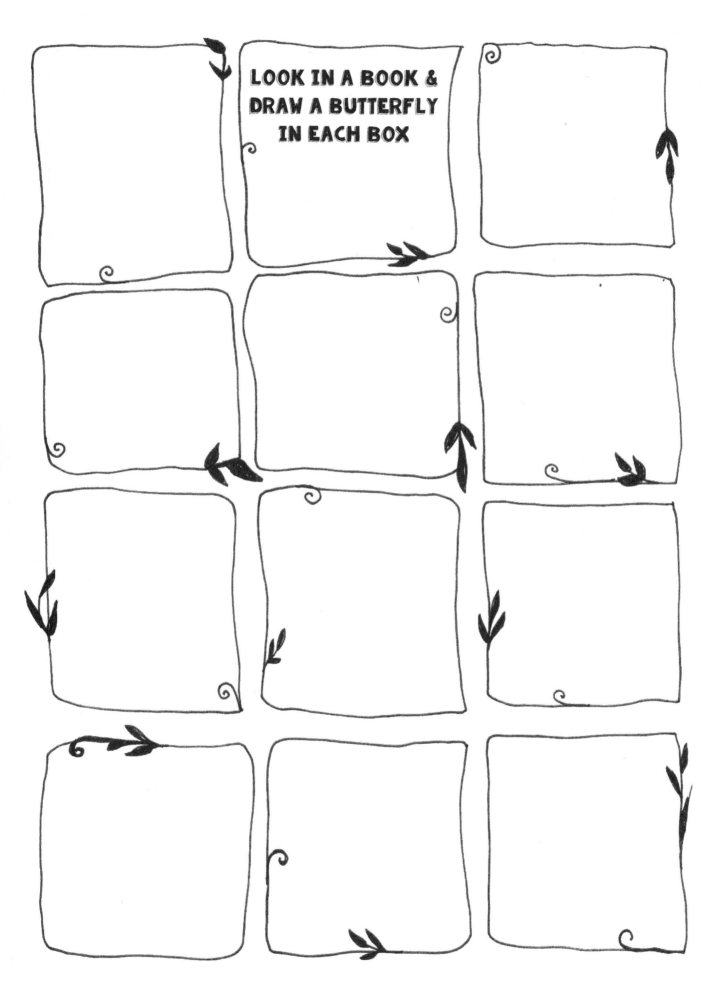

ADD SOMETHING TO THIS DRAWING

DESIGN A GARDEN

Today's Date:

COLOR ME
DRAW MY FOOD & HABITAT

LEARN MORE ABOUT FROGS & TOADS

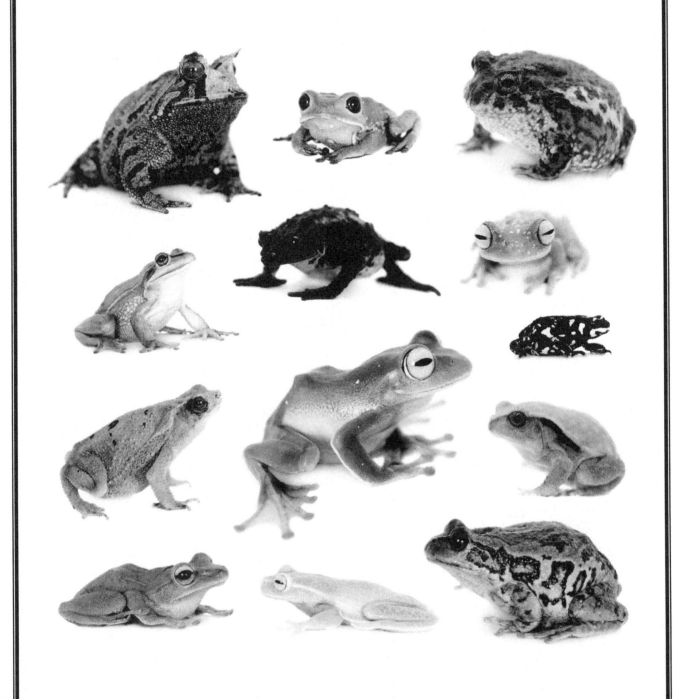

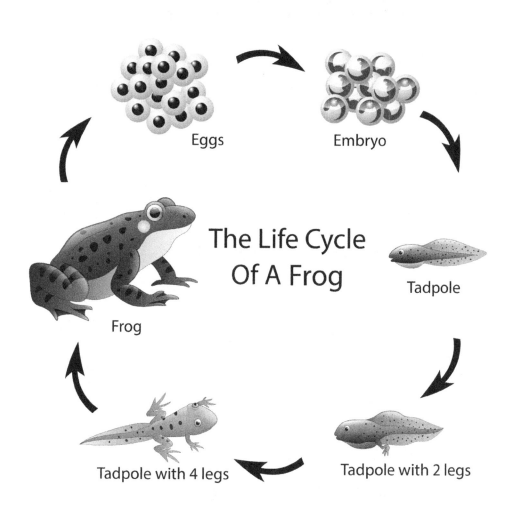

The Life Cycle Of A Frog

Eggs → Embryo → Tadpole → Tadpole with 2 legs → Tadpole with 4 legs → Frog

Five Facts About Frogs and Toads:

1. _____
2. _____
3. _____
4. _____
5. _____

LEARN ABOUT NATURE, WEATHER OR ANIMALS ON A DIFFERENT CONTINENT

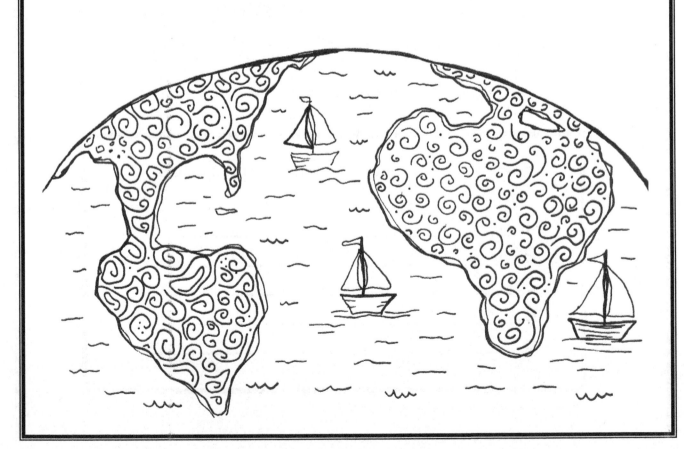

BIRDS OF THE WORLD

What bird are you learning about?
_____

Draw a Male

Draw a Female

Color the parts of the world where this bird lives.

COLLECT 10 SMALL THINGS FROM NATURE AND MAKE A NATURE CRAFT.

DRAW SMALL THINGS YOU SEE OUTSIDE

RESEARCH YOUR FAVORITE ANIMAL

SPELLING TIME

Choose a Plant or Animal & Draw it Below

_____

Look in your nature books for 5 words that have some of the same letters as this plant or animal.

1. _____
2. _____
3. _____
4. _____
5. _____

CHANGING WITH THE SEASONS
DRAW A _____
Show how it changes with each season.

GO OUTSIDE AND DRAW THE SKY

NATURE NOTES, QUOTES AND POETRY

USE A CAMERA TO TAKE PICTURES OF NATURE

Print your photos and place them here:

WATCH A DOCUMENTARY OR READ A BOOK ABOUT THE ANIMALS THAT LIVE IN FORESTS.

COLLECT 10 SMALL THINGS FROM YOUR YARD AND MAKE A NATURE CRAFT.

DRAW A PICTURE TO ILLUSTRATE THIS POEM

Recollections of Early Childhood

There was a time when meadow, grove, and stream,
The earth, and every common sight to me did seem
    Appareled in celestial light,
The glory and the freshness of a dream.

William Wordsworth

LEARN ABOUT NATURE, WEATHER OR ANIMALS ON A DIFFERENT CONTINENT

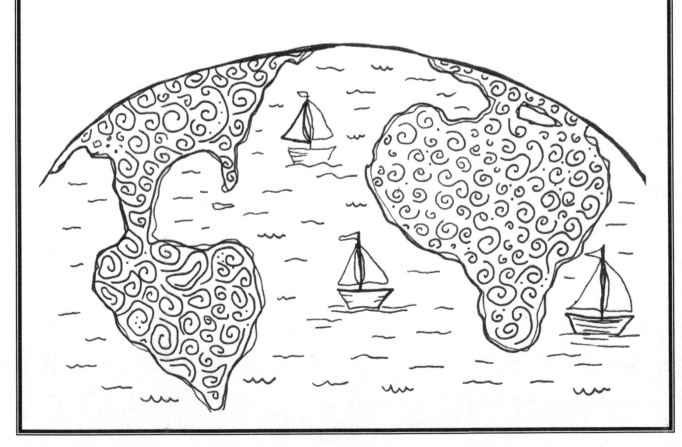

FOREST ANIMALS OF THE WORLD

What forest animal are you learning about?
_____

Draw a Male

Draw a Female

Color the parts of the world where this animal lives.

RESEARCH TREES.

Today's Date:
_____
_____

READING TIME

COLOR ME
DRAW MY FOOD & HABITAT

MOVIE TIME

Watch a movie or documentary about nature.

TITLE:_____

VOCABULARY BUILDING

Look in your Nature & Animal Books for **FOUR** words with more than **TEN** letters. Write the words and their definitions below:

LEARN ABOUT NATURE, WEATHER OR ANIMALS ON A DIFFERENT CONTINENT

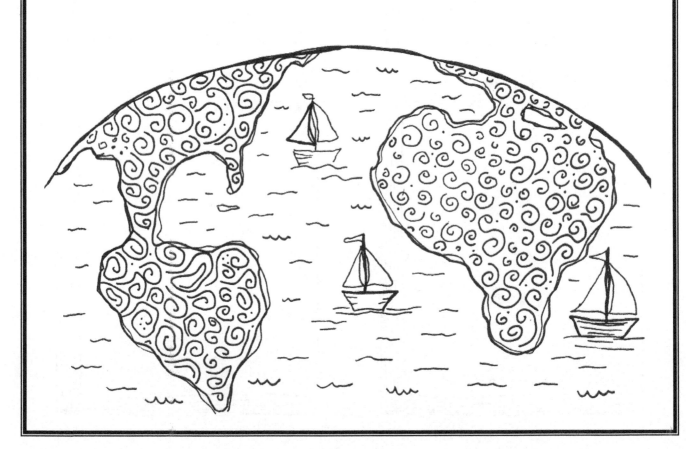

PLANTS OF THE WORLD

What plant are you learning about?

Draw it in Spring

Draw it in Autumn

Color the parts of the world where this plant lives.

NATURE NOTES, QUOTES AND POETRY

LEARN MORE ABOUT INSECTS

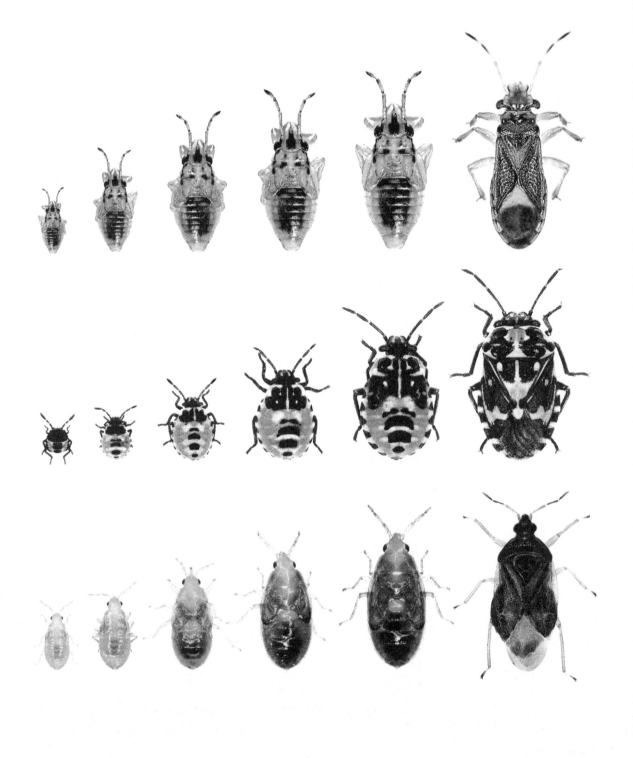

Five Facts About Insects:

1._____
2._____
3._____
4._____
5._____

COLLECT 10 SMALL THINGS FROM NATURE AND MAKE A NATURE CRAFT.

DRAW SMALL THINGS YOU SEE OUTSIDE

Today's Date:

READING TIME

COLOR ME
DRAW MY FOOD & HABITAT

SPELLING TIME

Choose a Plant or Animal & Draw it Below

_____

Look in your nature books for 5 words that have some of the same letters as this plant or animal.

1._____
2._____
3._____
4._____
5._____

CHANGING WITH THE SEASONS
DRAW A _____

Show how it changes with each season.

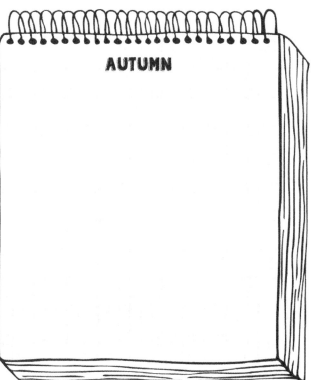

WATCH A DOCUMENTARY OR READ A BOOK ABOUT THE ANIMALS THAT LIVE IN OCEANS AND TIDE POOLS.

LEARN ABOUT NATURE, WEATHER OR ANIMALS ON A DIFFERENT CONTINENT

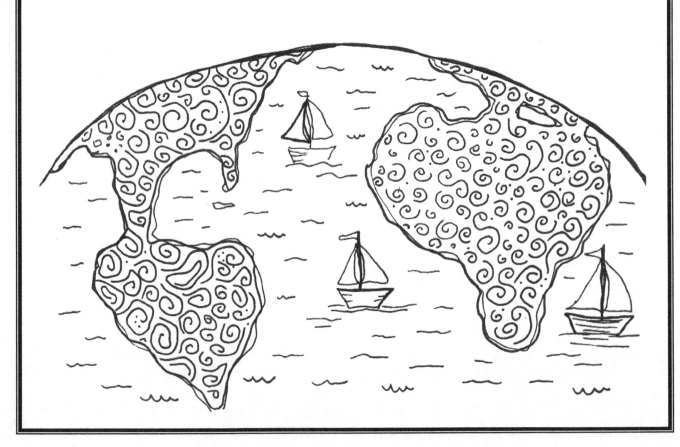

OCEAN ANIMALS OF THE WORLD

What ocean animal are you learning about?
_____

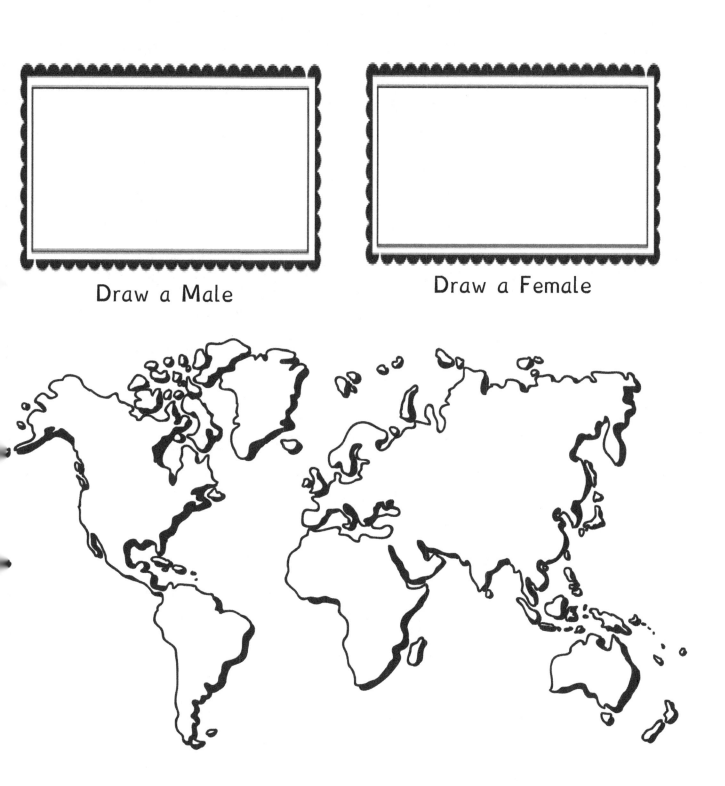

Draw a Male					Draw a Female

Color the parts of the world where this animal lives.

COLLECT 10 SMALL THINGS FROM YOUR YARD AND MAKE A NATURE CRAFT.

DRAW A PICTURE TO ILLUSTRATE THIS POEM

Recollections of Early Childhood

The rainbow comes and goes,
And lovely is the rose;
The moon doth with delight
Look round her when the heavens are bare;
Waters on a starry night
Are beautiful and fair;

William Wordsworth

RESEARCH YOUR FAVORITE BIRD

RESEARCH SOMETHING YOU SEE OUTSIDE TODAY.

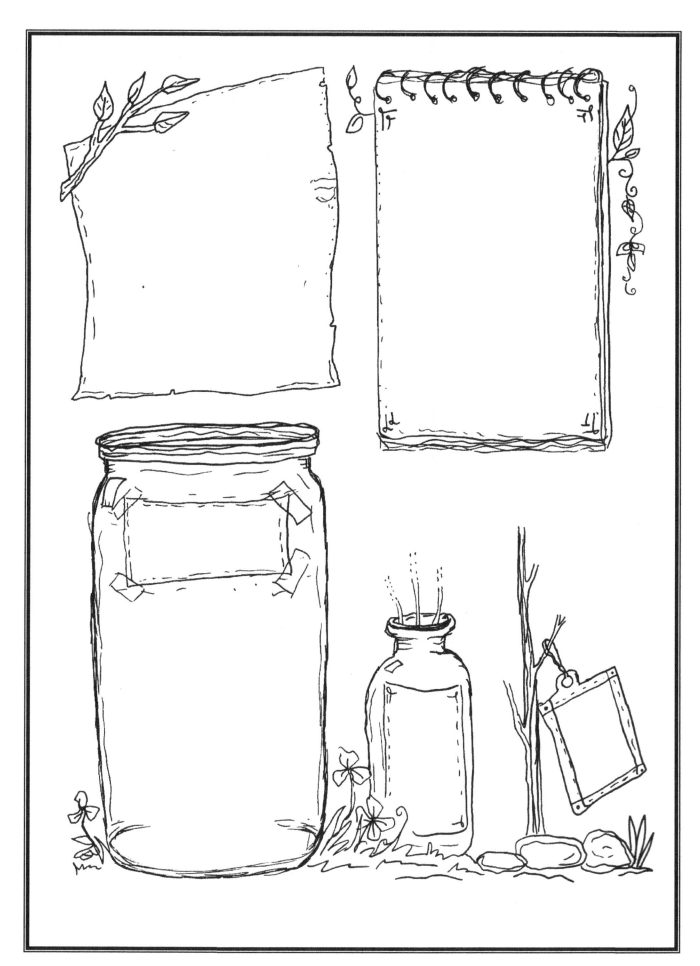

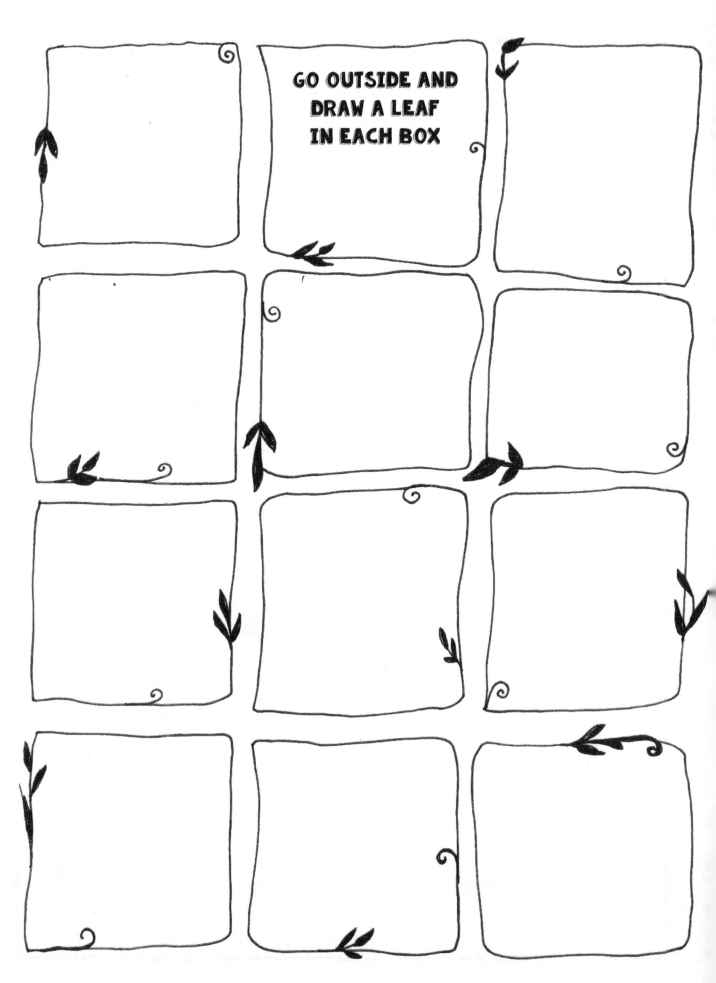

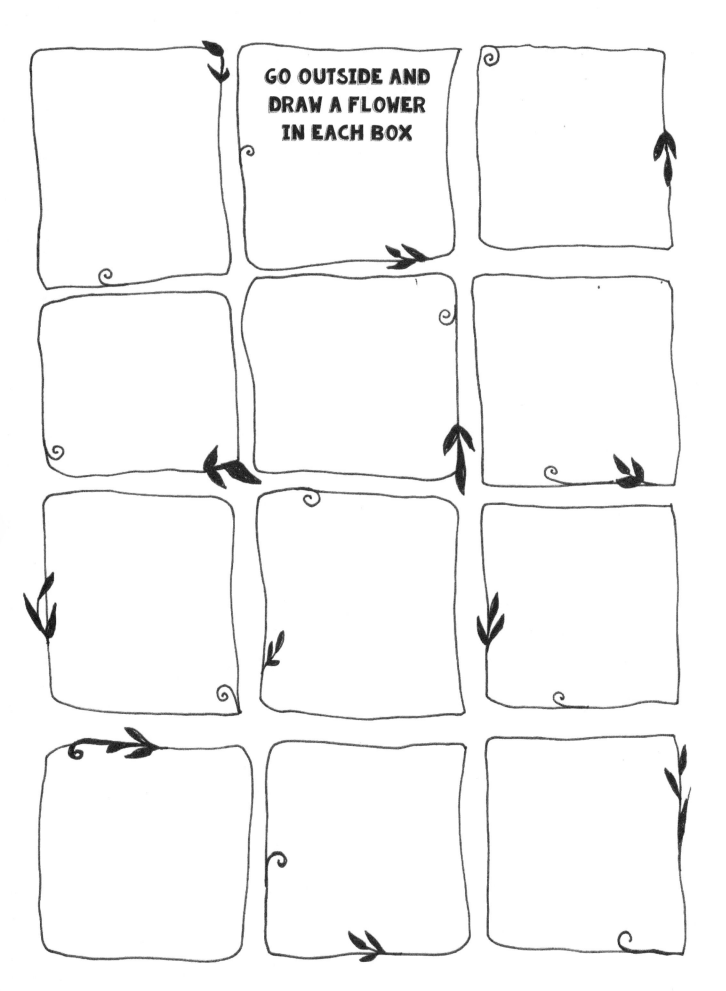

GO OUTSIDE AND DRAW THE SKY

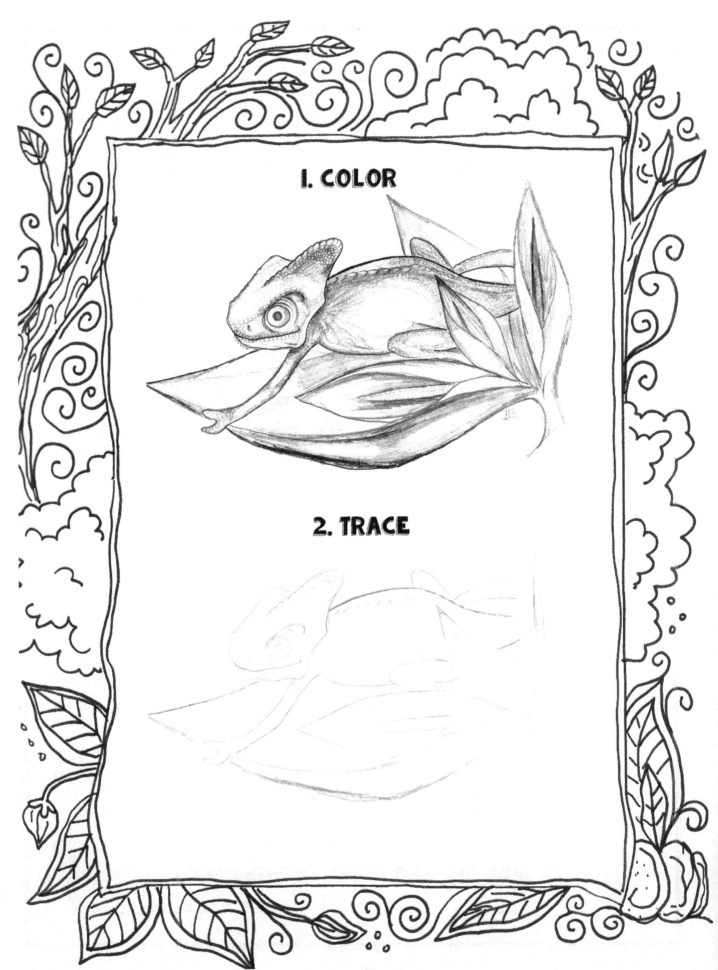

Today's Date:

READING TIME

COLOR ME
DRAW MY FOOD & HABITAT

THE REST OF THIS BOOK
IS WORDLESS

You can decide how to use each page.
Be creative, write, draw, color and think about
what you see, feel and hear outside.

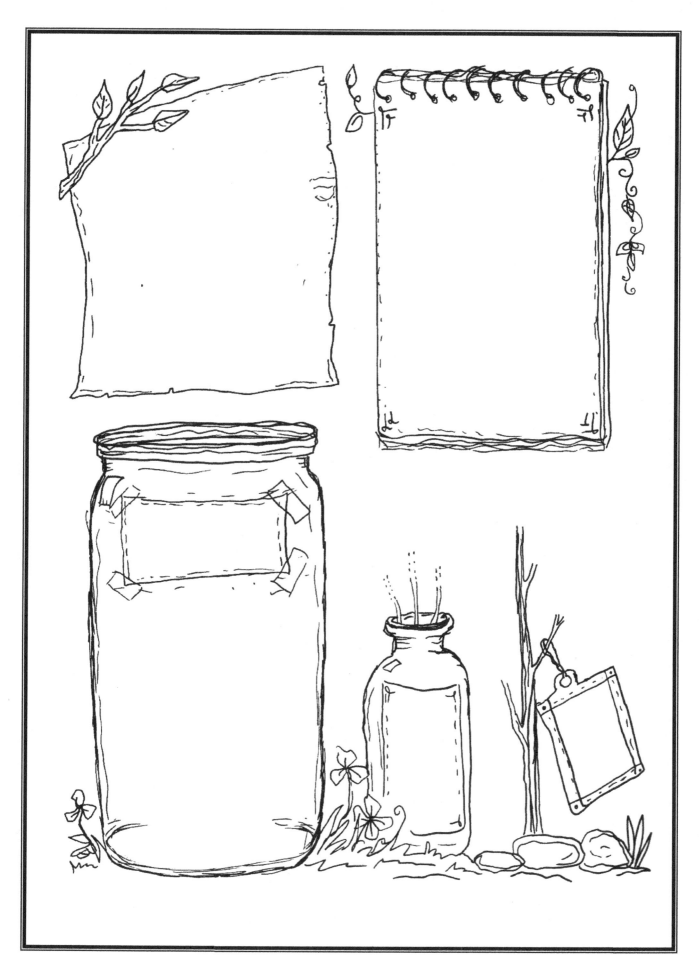

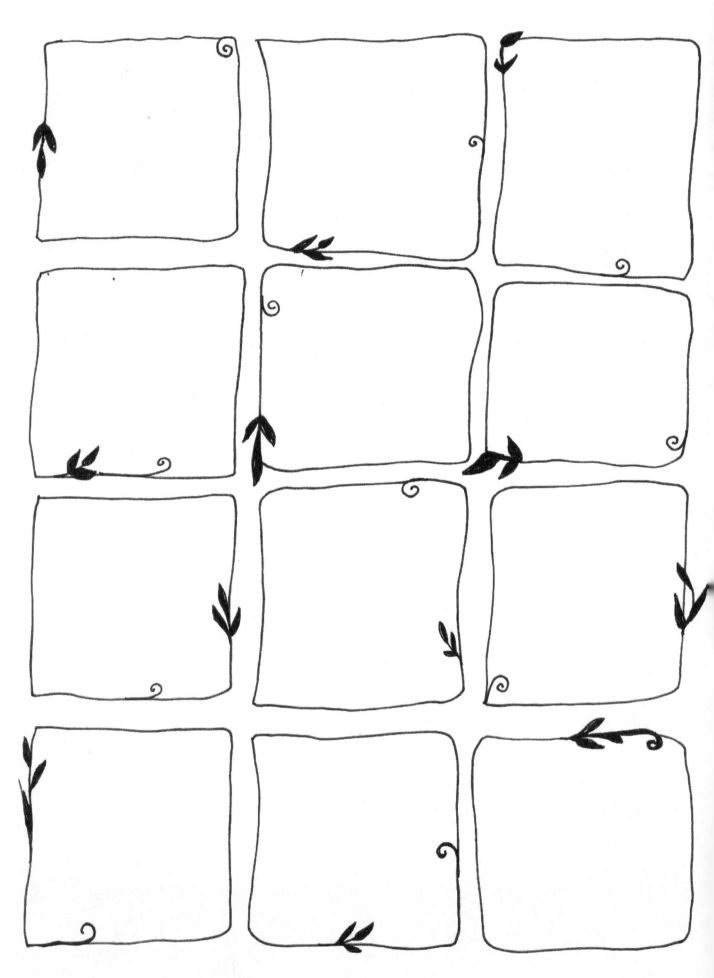

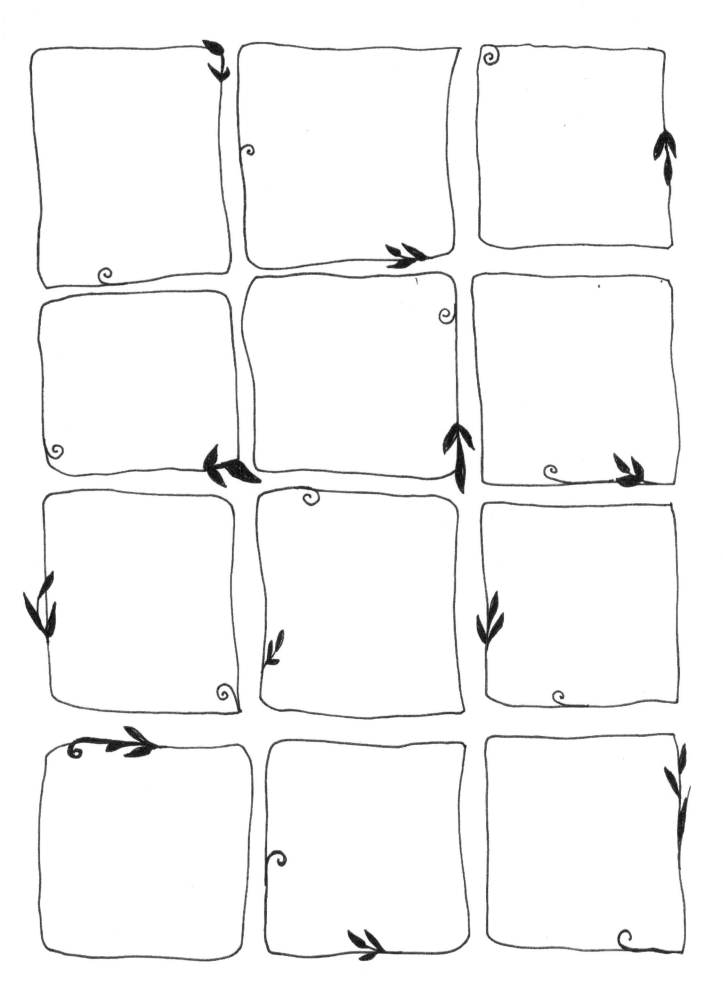

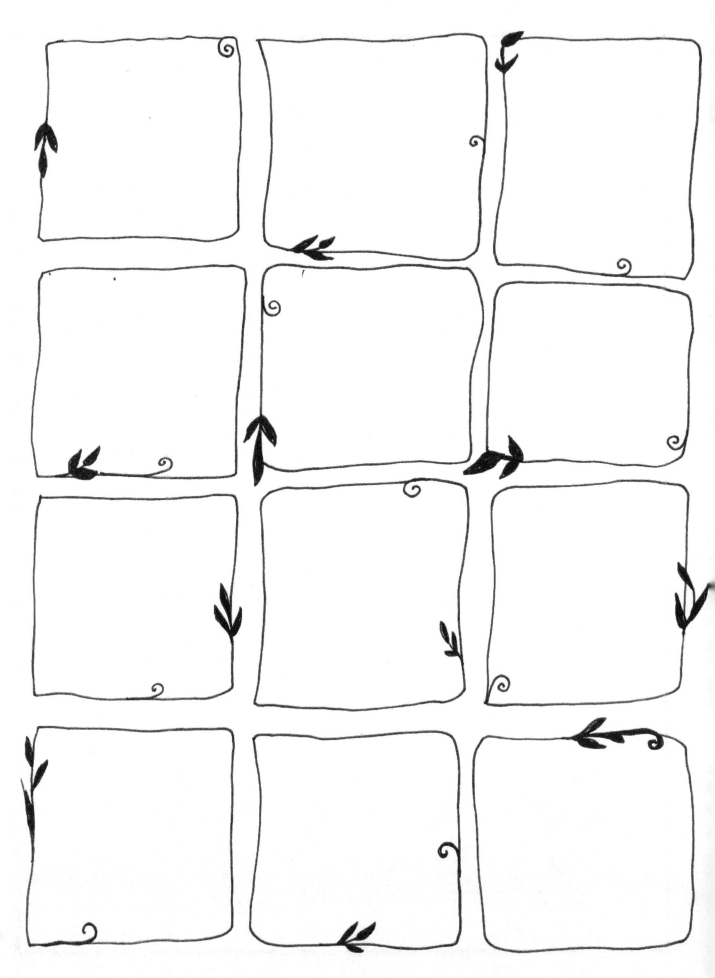

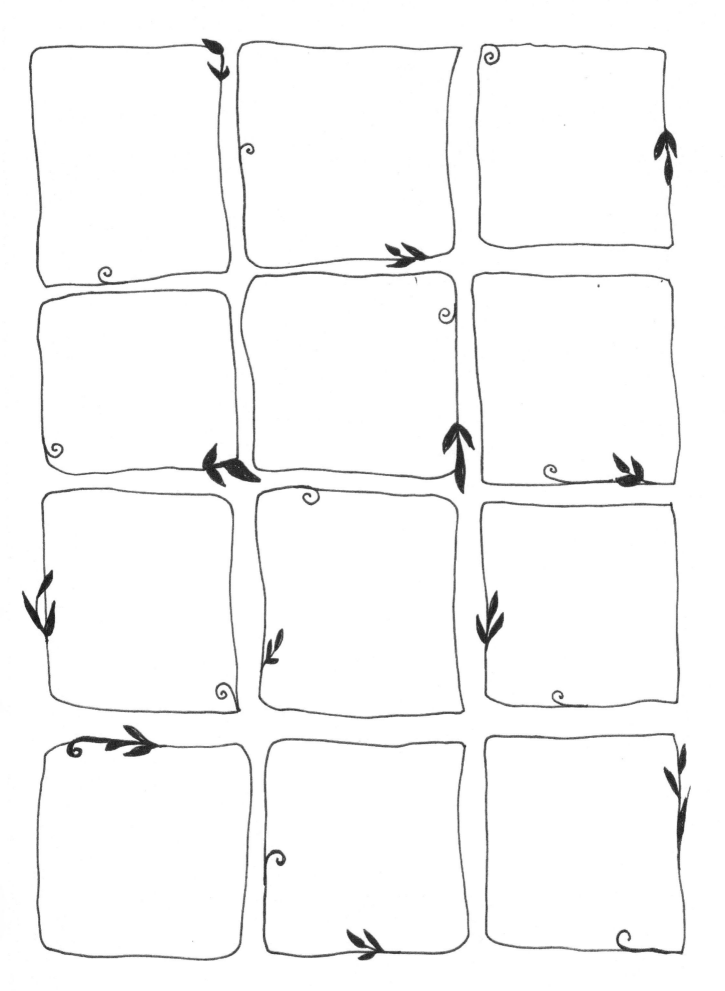

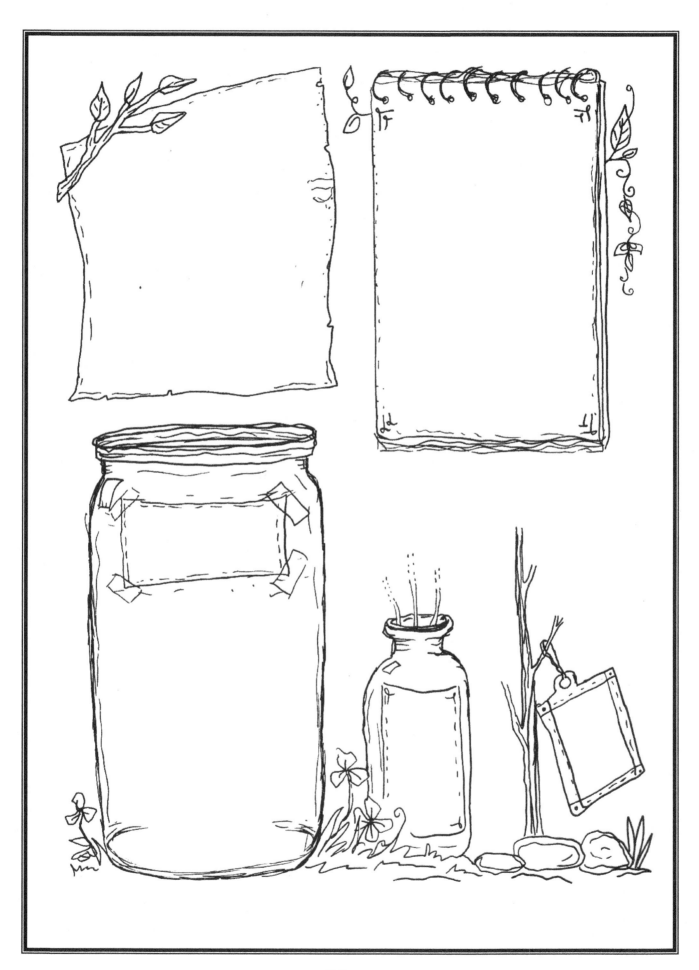

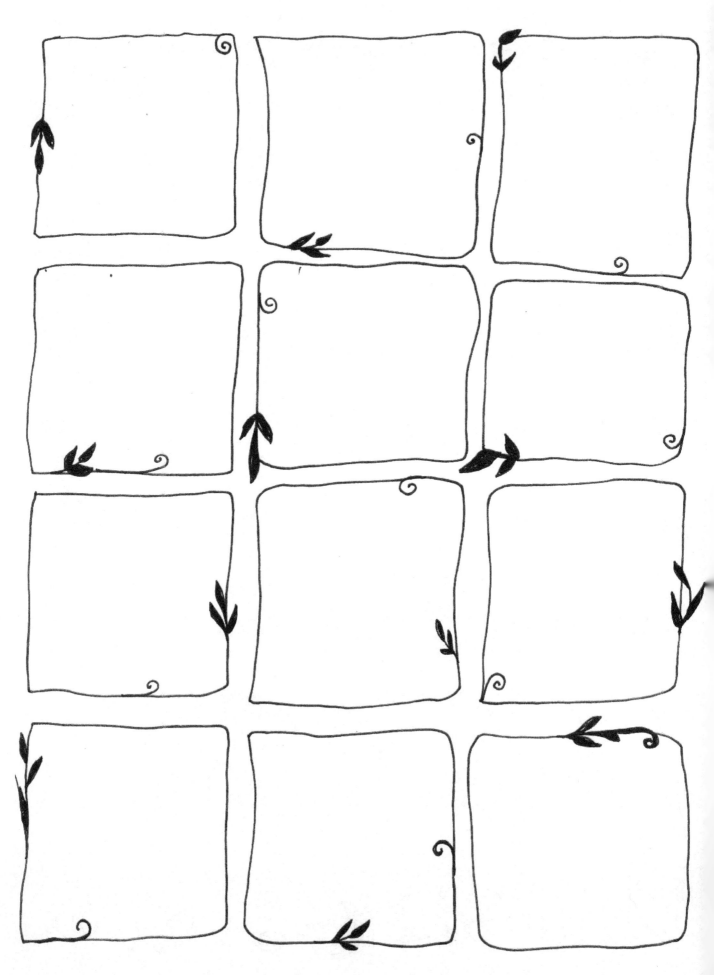

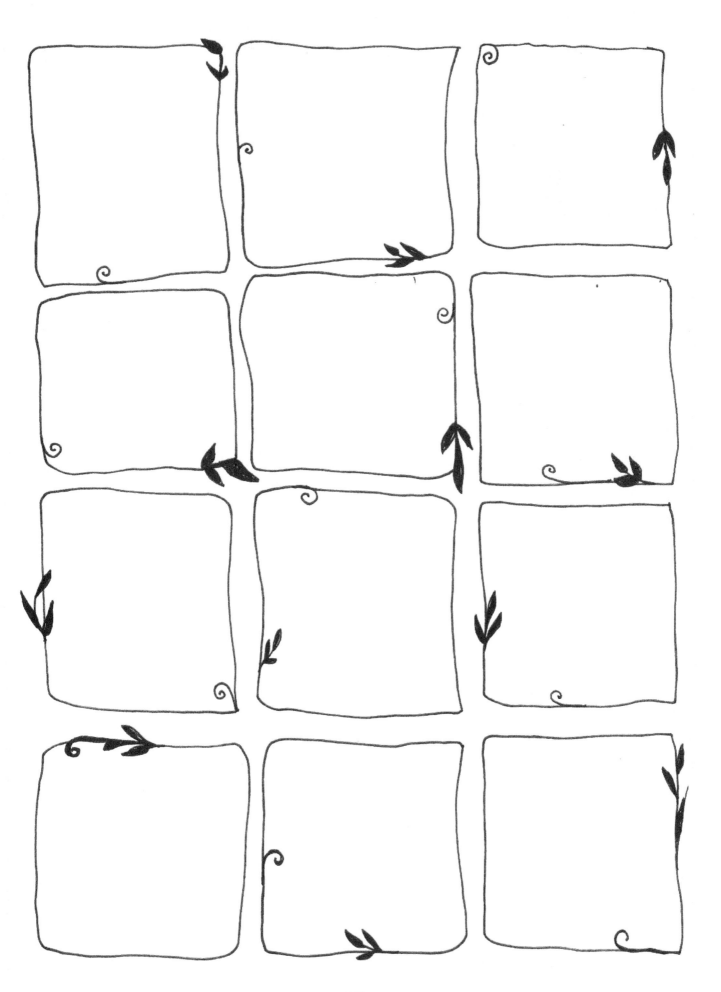

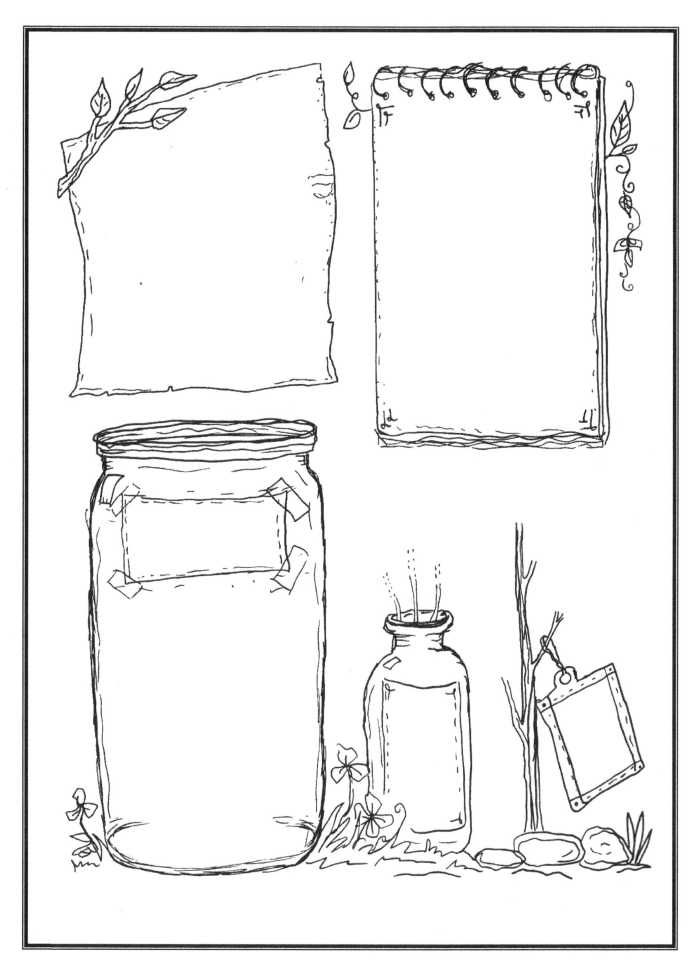

Made in the USA
Coppell, TX
28 April 2022